Taking A Stroll
❧ *with* ❧
MR. SIDE WALKER

Taking A Stroll

 *with*

MR. SIDE WALKER

"A Book of Poetry, Rhyme, & Song"

DAMIEN WALKER

To order additional copies of this book, contact:
Xlibris LLC
1-888-795-4274
www.Xlibris.com
Orders@Xlibris.com
128689

Contents

Reborn

MR. AND MRS. WALKER WERE PROUD
TO ANNOUNCE THE BIRTH OF A SON.

WHO SOME RECOGNIZE AS A PRODIGAL ONE.

RE-BORN AT TWENTY-EIGHT,
DISPLAYING EXTRAORDINARY TALENTS.

HE WROTE HOW ALL EXISTENCE BEGUN.
SOME IRRITATED,
BUT FASCINATED,
OF HOW HIS VOICE REVERBERATED.

HE WAS SURE TO HAVE LEFT YOUR EARS STUNNED.

HIS WORKS ELEVATED,
PRODUCING ASSETS THAT LIQUIDATED
HIS ENTIRE WORTH YET,
COULD EVER BE SPUN
FOR THOSE THAT GRAVITATED
TOWARDS THE FLOWS HE NARRATED.
THEY STRUCK A PAUSE
AT JUST HIS MENTION.

"DAMIEN?"

THE ROUTE HE NAVAGATED,
LEFT MOST QUITE AGGRAVATED.

HE WAS WARPED
AND BLOWN INTO THE NEXT DIMENSION.

The Big Bang

IN THE BEGINNING,
A FORCE CONTAINING
THREE HUNDRED SEXTILLION
CELESTIAL BODIES AFAR
BURSTS AND DISPERSES
STARS, PLANETS, AND MOONS.

A CELESTIAL BODY,
MOTIONS THROUGH SPACE,
STEADILY BURNING ITSELF TO EXHAUST.

IT DECREASES.
ITS SPIN RELEASES
GAS FROM WITHIN
AS IT SUDDENLY ROTATES AT A HALT.

VAPORS RISE AND EXPAND
PRODUCING CLOUDS OF PRECIPITATION
WHICH RAPIDLY COVERS ITS DOME.

A VISIBLE BODY,
FALLS FROM THE SKY
COVERING SEVENTY-TWO PERCENT
OF WHAT'S SHOWN.

CHANNELS OF AIR,
DERIVE FROM ITS SURFACE,
MAKING WAVES
THE FIRST TO HAVE BLOWN.

A LIQUID LIKE SUBSTANCE,
ATTACHED AND COMBINED,
COMPELLING THE MAKING OF CLONES.

SWEPT SEEDS,
SPROUT FLOWERS AND TREES
CHIRPING, ARE THOSE SOON TO HAVE FLOWN.

A FETUS,
PUSHED BY ITS TIDE,
BARE WITNESS WITH EYES
CONSTRUCTED WITHIN SKELETAL BONE.

EGGS BURST,
SWIMMING IN SCHOOLS ARE VERTEBRATES,
WHICH BREATHED THROUGH THEIR GILLS.

OTHER LIFE
IS RELEASED FROM A SLIT,
OBTAINING ITS BREATH AS IT SPILLS.

QUAKES, SLOWLY BEGIN TO TREMBLE
AS MOUNTAINS OF DIRT AND ICE
BEGIN TO FORM.

PUNCHES OF MELTED ROCK
LAY WITH HIDDEN
BENEATH ITS SURFACE,
HEATED BY THE SOURCE OF IT'S CORE.

RADIATION,
NOURISHES ITS LIFE BY DAY,
AS THE NIGHT SENDS OFF
IT'S GRAVITATIONAL PULL.

LET'S NOW TURN THE PAGE,
TAKE A LOOK AT THE DAY OF FINALLY
WHEN THE EARTH STOOD STILL.

The Alignment of the Planets

SHATTERED GLASS
FELL ONTO STREET PAVEMENTS
OF WORLD WIDE SYNAGOGUES.

RICOCHETING AND PIERCING THE SKIN
OF OUTSIDE DEVIL WORSHIPERS.

PRAYING THEIR PRINCE OF DARKNESS,
WOULD OVER POWER THE LIGHT,
WHICH WAS NOW SHINING UPON THEM.

THE END OF ALL DAYS WAS NOW HERE,
SENDING PREACHERS
AND CLERGY TRAMPLING
THROUGH THE STREETS
SMOTHERED IN VIRGINS BLOOD.

SHOWCASING,
THEIR MARK OF THE SECOND COMING.

SPARKING PAUSE,
FROM THOSE WHOM STOOD TO WITNESS
THE HEAVENS RELEASE STRIKING ANGELS,
VANQUISHING DEMONIC POSSESSIONS
RETAINED WITHIN
THE THRESHOLDS OF THEIR SINS.

SQUELCHING FLESH,
DEMINISHED TO ASHES
BLOWING INTO SKELETAL REMAINS
PROTRUDING FROM SMOKING GRAVES.

PERISHING BONES,
INTO THE MIST OF SWELTERING SAND STORMS.

SWEEPING ACROSS ENTIRE NATIONS.

WHILE MISFITS CHANNELED NUCLEAR EXPLOSIONS
TO EXEMPLIFY AND BEGIN DUPLICATING,
SEPARATE ATROCITIES.

STAGING
UNWARRANTED GENOCIDES.

SHAKING AND SINKING CONTINENTS
AT, WHICH TIME.

Revelations

THE CORE OF THE EARTH
HAD CEASED TO BUBBLE,
AS IT DISCONTINUED IN ITS ROTATION.

HALF OF THE PLANET
REMAINED COLD IN THE DARK,
AS THE REMAINING CONTAINED
THE SUN'S RADIATION.

LAVA SPURTED
THROUGH VOLCANO TOPS,
AS ICE CAPS BEGAN TO MELT.

MUDSLIDES HAD BEGUN TO OCCUR
AS AVALANCHES STEADILY FELL.

HURRICANES,
TORNADOES,
CLOUDS,
AND BIRDS
DISCONTINUED TO EXIST IN THE SKY.

THERE WAS NO LONGER
COOL BREEZES OF AIR.
IT WAS AS IF THE WIND HAD JUST DIED.

THOUSAND FOOT WAVES,
WASHED UP ON SHORES,
CRUSHING EVERYTHING IN ITS PATH.

LIFE CONSUMED.
DECEASED WERE BILLIONS.
THERE WAS NO QUESTION
IF THIS WAS GOD'S WRATH.

CONCEALED IN THE DARKNESS,
WERE THE SUN
WAS NO LONGER FOUND TO GLOW.

RAIN,
HAIL,
SLEET,
AND SNOW
TOOK BY STORM,
THIS PORTION OF THE GLOBE.

TREES SHATTERED LIKE GLASS,
AS GLACIERS SHOOK
UNTIL THEY CRACKED INTO PIECES.

ANIMALS AND PEOPLE
WERE FROZEN IN ICE.
THEIR EYES FIXATED
LIKE TRUE BELIEVERS.

HALF OF THE WORLD,
WAS SET ON FIRE,
AS THE REMAINING,
WAS FROZEN SPILLS.

STARS AND PLANETS,
CAME TOGETHER AS ONE,
BY THE FORCE
OF THAT MIGHTY ONE'S WILL.

THOUSANDS OF RAINBOWLIKE BRIDGES,
WERE RELEASED,
FROM THIS HUMONGOUS ENERGY OF LIGHT.

SOULS BY THE MILLIONS,
BEGAN THEIR ASCENSION,
PREPARED FOR WHAT WAS KNOWN AS A FLIGHT.

WITH THE FINAL SOULS GATHERED ON,
THERE WAS NOTHING LEFT BUT EMPTY SPACE.

THE PARADISE BALL OF ENERGY WHISKED OFF,
NOT LEAVING ANY EVIDENCE NOR TRACE.

FROM THE EARTH'S ALTERNATION
OF BEING SO HOT
AND YET SO COLD.

THE EARTH'S SURFACE
BEGAN TO BREAK AWAY,
FINALLY BEGUN TO EXPLODE.

EXPLOSIONS HAD BEGUN TO CEASE,
AS WHAT WAS LET OFF,
WAS IT'S FINAL *BOOM*!

WHAT REMAINED OF THE EARTH,
POSITIONED IN SPACE,
WAS NOW LEFT
IN THE FORM OF A MOON.

Mr. Side Walker

SIDE WALKERS,
WALKING IN THE DOORS OF A MOSQUE,
BEING HANDED A HOLY QURAN,
RECEIVING INSTRUCTIONS FROM ALLAH! LAH! LAH! LAH!
LAH! LAH! LAH!

SIDE WALKERS,
PEDDLING PRESCRIPTIVE MEDICATIONS ON THE STREET!

SIDE WALKERS,
CHANNELING STATIONS,
DISPLAYING SOME NEW HEAT.
SWITCHED UP THE GAME BECAME A COP.
WATCHED THAT FIREMAN JUST DROP.

SIDE WALKERS,
TUMBLING FROM OFF OF A BUILDING
INTO THE STREET.

SIDE WALKERS,
EAGERLY READY,
PUMPING LIKE SOMETHING SWEET.
IT WAS BATTERY ACID
THAT LACED THAT SHOT.
THAT CAUSED YOU TO LAY
IN THAT BIG PINE BOX.

SIDE WALKERS,
CASH CARDS FLOSSING,
MINKS WITH BIG DIAMOND RINGS.

SIDE WALKERS,
LUXURY CARS AND HOMES,
THAT WERE CUSTOM MADE.
BROUGHT DOWN THE GATE
AND CLOSED UP SHOP.
NOW TWO DECADES,
BEEN ON LOCK.

SIDE WALKERS,
FOREVER READY,
ACCEPTING A NEW FEAT.

SIDE WALKERS,
STEADY,
READY,
STOMPING A NEW BEAT.
WE REP OUT IN VA AT DIFFERENT SPOTS
OR UP AT MORNINGWEST SIDE PARK.

SIDE WALKERS,
WE SHOW UP LARGE,
WHEN FAITH IS IN CHARGE.

SIDE WALKERS,
WE BELIEVE IN GOD.
SO WE COMING HARD.
THE ENTIRE FAMILY,
COME TO PARTY.
SO, LETS GET DANCING WITH THEM STARS.

SIDE WALKERS,
WHERE MY NUBIAN PRINCESS?
MY NEFER FER TEE-TEE.

SIDE WALKERS,
MY CAUCASIAN,
ASIAN,
LATIN,
MAKING THAT MONEY.

SIDE WALKERS,
LOOKING MUMMIFIED,
WALKING ON WALLSTREET,
WEARING MAKE UP LIKE HALLOWEEN,
PAINTED FACES ON T.V.

SIDE WALKERS,
DEMONSTRATING,
IN THE CAPITAL OF NEW YORK.

SIDE WALKERS,
CHASTISING LEGISLATORS,
DEMANDING REAL TALK.

SIDE WALKERS,
JUST WON APPEALS,
GOT BAILED OUT OF COURT,
OFF THE TARGET RANGE,
GOOD SPORT,
DROPPED THOSE STINKING, THINKING THOUGHTS.

SIDE WALKERS,
TEXTING MESSAGES
USING CELLULAR PHONES.

SIDE WALKERS,
WHO CRASHED A PLANE,
JUST LANDED A DRONE,
BLOWN OFF A HIGH-WAY
IN A MOBILE HOME,
LOST HIS FAMILY IN ROADSIDE BOMBS.

SIDE WALKERS,
WHO JUST LOST THEIR KIDS
AND STARTED A BID.

SIDE WALKERS,
WHO JUST BOUGHT A CRIB
AND LEARNED HOW TO LIVE,

GOT MARRIED,
SNATCHED A GIG
NOW THROUGH COLLEGE ARE HIS KIDS.

SIDE WALKERS! WALKER! WALKER! WALKER! WALKER!

SIDE WALKERS! WALKER! WALKER! WALKER! WALKER!

SSSIIIDE WALKERS!!!!

Smoking Hills

NEVER SUCH A VISION
ARISEN WITHIN HIS MIND.

MILITANTS STRAPPED UP
WITH AN ARSENAL OF EVERY KIND.

CAMOUFLAGED ON MOUNTAIN TOPS,
CREEPING IN BEHIND.

THE ENEMY NEVER SAW WHAT WAS COMING
UNTIL ONE STEPPED ON A MINE.

FINGERS FELL ON TRIGGERS,
AS BODIES BEGAN BLOWING TO PIECES.

GRENADES BEGAN RELEASING THE AIR,
FILLED WITH HEAT SEEKERS.

BULLETS RIPPED THROUGH BODIES,
AS THEY TUMBLED AND FELL.

VICTIMS PROCEEDED TO LOOK UP,
AT THESE OPPOSING REBELS THEMSELVES.

THEIR THROATS WERE BEING SLIT,
ONLY TO SILENCE THEIR YELLS.

EXPLOSIONS SHATTERED EARDRUMS,
ONLY BLOOD COULD BE SMELLED.

SKULL REMAINS WERE CRUSHED,
AS SWORDS WERE DRIVEN THROUGH HEARTS.

BODIES LIED EITHER BEHEADED
OR RELINQUISHED OF PARTS.

THE MIST OF GUNPOWDER,
SLOWLY SETTLED TO THE GROUND.

AND JUST LIKE ANY OTHER GRAVE YARD,
YOU NO LONGER HEARD A SOUND.

The Last Stop

ROBBED SOULFULLY
OF MY MENTAL,
ABSORBED INTO,
THE PHYSICAL THINGS
THAT NEGLECTS MY EMOTIONS.

BLIND,
TRAPPED,
OUT OF CONTROL.

RUNNING THROUGH MAIN STREETS AND TRACKS.
LIKE A TRAIN WITH NO BRAKES,
I'M HEADED TOWARDS
THE END OF MY LINE.

MY NURTURE ALONG THE WAY,
WAS MUCH LESS THAN
WHAT IT SHOULD BE.

SO MY SEEDS WHISTLED
WITH LEAVES IN THE WIND.

MY SENSES BECAME
SHUT DOWN WITHIN.

MY OXYGEN LEVEL,
NO LONGER THICK BUT THIN.

ITS GETTING HOT
AND MY ENGINES ABOUT TO BLOW.

BUT HOW WILL MY SEEDS KNOW
HOW TO GROW?
IF THE SEEDS FROM WHICH THEY CAME
FROM DIDN'T KNOW?
SIDE BARS AND DOORS,
NOW OPEN AND CLOSE.

SPARKS OF FLAME,
SLOWLY BRINGS THINGS TO A STOP.
MY SEEDS' SEEDS
NOW HAVE GROWN,
GROWN FROM WHICH WAY THEY DROPPED.

MY SEEDS' SEED,
HAS ARISEN WITH ROOTS,
ROOTS FROM THE SON WHOM RESIDES
WITH THE SON IN THE SKY.

I WILL LOVE MY SEEDS' SEED
NOW, ALWAYS AND FOREVER.

I WILL LOVE HIM,
THE DAY AFTER THE DAY,
AFTER THE DAY THAT I DIE

"ALL ABOARD!"
LET'S RIDE

THE TOKEN IS ON ME.

Capital Punishment

PARALYZED IN THE COLD,
REFLECTIONS OF BONE COLLECTORS.

VULTURES LERKING WITHIN THE DARK,
INSTITUTIONALIZED IN MEN'S CORRECTIONS
WITH SOLE INTENTIONS
OF STRIVING TO CONVINCE THE COURTS.

PETRIFIED,
AWOKEN,
SWEATING,
COUNTING BLESSINGS,
A CONCOCTION STOPS HIS HEART.

PENALIZED LIKE THOSE SUBJECTED TO DEATH ROW EXITS,
IN A PUDDLE HE LEFT HIS MOMS.

TRAUMATIZED AT CLOSING SESSIONS
OF DOSED INJECTIONS,
THERE WAS A STRUGGLE TO KEEP HER CALM.

TERRIFIED OF EXPOSING
EXTRAS TO THOSE PROJECTIONS,
THEY HUDDLED TO RESTRAIN HER ARMS.

AUTHORIZED IN THEIR SELECTIONS
TO HOLD CRUEL PROFESSIONS,
THOSE STICKS WERE SOME HOW DRAWN.

DEMONSTRATED WAS GROSS DISCRETIONS,
IN THEIR ELECTION,
DESPITE HER BELLY TO USE BATONS.

From the Cradle to the Grave

CHOSEN ARE THOSE BORN,
STILL OR ADDICTED AS A FETUS.

SOME, BURIED IN TRASH CANS,
WHERE NURTURE WAS NEEDED.

OTHERS, STRUCK BY BULLETS POISONED,
DROWNED, FATALLY BURNED.

SUFFICATED BY PARENT'S ORDEALS
PAINFULLY LEARNED.

SOME ARE CHOSEN
TO BE MISGUIDED BY FOOLS.

ONLY VALUES THEY POSSESS
ARE SIMPLE DIAMONDS AND JEWELS.

NO PRINCIPLES AT ALL,
MIS-USING THEIR SCHOOLS.

AS A PLACE WHERE THEY HUSTLE
AND CARRY THE WRONG TOOLS.

SUBJECTED TO IGORANCE,
CAUGHT UP IN A STRUGGLE,
SOME ARE CHOSEN TO O.D.,
CRASH-DRUNK,
OR CUT THEIR OWN JUGULARS.

DESTINED TO FEEL THE PAIN
AND WHO WILL FEEL IT WORST.

THE BODY THAT CRIES OVER THE COFFIN
OR THE ONE THAT RIDES IN A HEARSE.

CALL IT BAD CHOICES
OR CALL IT A CURSE,
I'M JUST PRAYING THAT IGNORANCE
HAS NOT CAUSED YOU TO HEAR IT HERE FIRST.

HISTORY WITH HOLDS LESSONS
THAT ARE CONSTANTLY UNFOLDING.

ALL YOU HAVE TO FIGURE OUT IS
EXACTLY FOR WHAT
YOU WERE CHOSEN.

CHOSEN ONE.

The Day of Reckoning

I DON'T WANNA LEAVE A LEGACY
CONVEYING THE GHETTO GOT THE BEST OF ME.

SO I'M PRAYING THAT
IT WAS JUST A TEST TO SEE.

IF I CREATED A BETTER DESTINY.

MY DAY OF ATONEMENT
LIED, TUCKED AWAY, FROZEN
IN DREAMS, CONCEIVED WHILE SLEEPING
IN DECREPIT BUILDINGS.

STAKED OUT BY RATS,
BIG AS CATS,
CREEPING THROUGH FLOOR BOARDS,
WALLS, AND THE CEILINGS.

HARBORING ROACHES IN PACKS,
COLLECTING THEIR SNACKS
OFF THE BACKS OF MILLIONS,
OF MALNOURISHED CHILDREN.

WHO RESORTED TO SELLING CRACK,
STRAYED OFF THE TRACK OF BECOMING
WORKING CLASS CITIZENS.

NEIGHBORHOOD WATCH,
PUSHED OUTSTOCK,
ROCKING THE BLOCK,
FOR LOCAL DOPE DEALERS.

WEIGHT WATCHERS WERE POPPED,
CUFFED UP BY NARCS,
AS BOOM BOXES PLAYED OUT
TUPAC AND BIG POPPA.

HOOKERS STRUNGOUT,
LOOKING FOR CLOUT,
ROUND ABOUT,
OPENED UP DOORS,
TO TRUCKS AND CAR STOPPERS.

SINGLE MOTHERS,
WAS THE MAJORITY LEADERS,
IN WELFARE OFFICES,
THAT WERE OVERCROWDED WITH MILLIONS OF POOR
PEOPLE.

SEARCHING FOR FOOD, FUND, AND AID,
TURNED AWAY IN DISMAY,
MOST COULD NO LONGER AFFORD EITHER.

DEATH AND TRAGEDY,
SPRUNG UP ALTERS,
WITH FLOWERS, CROSSES, AND PICTURES
ON STREET CORNERS.

WERE PARENTS STOOD SILENT,
CRIED KNEED, AND PRAYED,
MOURNING THE LOSSES OF SONS AND DAUGHTERS.

HOSPITALS, SOUP KITHCHENS, SCHOOLS
WERE RULED BY NEW WORLD ORDER.

MOST CHILDREN WERE TAUGHT
AND SPOON FED,
WHAT WAS IMPLEMENTED BY FOUR FATHERS.

IF YOU ASKED ME TO DESCRIBE,
MY YOUTH IN THE GHETTO,
I WOULD SAY IT WAS ALL TORTURE.
FOR ME TO LEAVE A STRONG LEGACY,
AT THIS POINT,
WOULD BE A TALL ORDER.

PERHAPS, I COULD CONTINUE WRITING BOOKS,
BECOME A WELL KNOWN AUTHOR.

BURY THESE CHAINS FROM WHERE I CAME,
MAKING MY WAY THROUGH ALL BORDERS.

I'M SURE THE CONDITIONS I SHARED HERE TODAY,
WILL BE ALL WELL THOUGHT OF.

BUT JUST REMEMBER,
THIS POEM WAS WRITTEN
FOR THOSE OF YOU WHO GREW UP,
DISTRAUGHT AND CAUGHT UP.

SO PLEASE, DON'T LEAVE A LEGACY,
CONVEYING THE GHETTO GOT THE BEST OF THEE.

JUST PRAY THAT IT WAS JUST A TEST TO SEE.

IF YOU CREATED A BETTER DESTINY.

Motivational Speaker

POWERFUL MINDS COLLABORATE THOUGHTS,
OF INSANE PLOTS
TO ASSASSINATE THOSE THAT POSSESS,
SUCH AN INFLUENTIAL MIND AS MYSELF.

MY TEACHINGS ARE PROTESTED AGAINST,
YET MY VIEWS ARE IRREFUTABLE.

I ERADICATE ANY DISBELIEF,
BY DEBATING AGAINST PROFESSIONALS.

I REINTEGRATE MINDS,
ABOLISHED BY SLAVERY,
I'M ABOLITIONARY SOLDIER!

FROM ABROAD AND BACK TO THE STATES,
DO YOU REMEMBER THE DOCUMENTARIES I SHOWED
YOU?

I'M PAYING THE COST OF SOMETHING NON-REFUNDABLE.
I'M HEADED TOWARDS BETRAYAL.

I'M RECEIVING MALICIOUS PHONE CALLS
AND RETRIEVING THREATENING MAIL.

MY HOME FRONT ISN'T SAFE,
NEITHER, IS MY CONGREGATION EITHER.

MY SCHEDULE MUST REMAIN,
AS IS MY PEOPLE ARE COUNTING ON ME TO BE THERE.

MY PLACE IS AT THIS PODIUM,
LOOKING AT FACES ALL SO FAMILIAR.

THAT YELL FROM A MAN,
DRAWING A GUN FROM HIS POCKET.

SEEMED MORE THAN A LITTLE PECULIAR.

I'M HERE TO MEET MY MAKER!

THE BULLETS RIPPED RIGHT THROUGH ME.
PLEASE LEAVE ME HERE.

LET ME REST
AND ALLOW YOUR WORDS TO MOVE ME.

MOTIVATIONAL SPEAKER!

Re-Course

FRUSTRATION AND CONFUSION,
DRAWS BLIND EYES TO NO SOLUTION.

WE ARE PARALYZED,
IN OUR DREAMS OF EVOLUTION.
AWOKEN,
ONLY TO REMAIN,
STAGNATED IN OUR MOVEMENTS.

WE ARE LOOKING,
FOR SOMEONE TO CALL ON,
TO CHANGE THE COURSE OF OUR FUTURE.

OUR CONSTITUTION,
WILL ONLY FROWN.
SHOULD WE APPOINT ANOTHER SUIT HERE?

WHO EMBRACES MONOPLY?
IS TICKLED BY MONOTONY?
FALLING HEAD OVER HEELS
IN HYPOCRISY,
TENDING TRIALS,
AS IF THERE MOCKERIES,
POSTING NUMBERS,
CALL IT LOTTERY.

PICK UP THE PHONE,
CALL ON DEMOCRACY.
ENQUIRE WITH THEM,
AS TO WHAT WILL OUR TOMORROW BRING.
PERHAPS, THEY'LL BE ON LINE WITH SECURITY,
ADDRESSING THOSE INCOMING CALLS ON OUR THERAPY.

WHERE IS IT IN
"CORRECTION"
DOES IT STATE THAT YOU BURY ME?
OR FORCE ME TO BEHAVE,
AS THOUGH I'M CRIPPLED,
WHEN I'VE REDEFINED MY MENTAL.
IT IS THE UPLIFTING,
WE MUST TEND TO.
IT'S NOT MY POSITION
TO OFFEND YOU.
THERE IS NO NEED TO AIM,
ANOTHER MISSILE,
WHEN IT IS AT HOME,
THAT WE HAVE ISSUES.
LET THE MONEY FOR THOSE ARMS,
BE PLACED INTO MORE OUTREACHING CENTERS,
FOR KIDS OF YOUR OWN.
OR PERHAPS, ONE THAT HAS BEEN MENTORED,
PUSH TOWARDS RECOURSE
AND CEASE ON ATTACKS,
WITH EVERY ETHINICITY,
WHETHER THEIR WHITE OR THEIR BLACK.

Thinking Things Over

YOU KNOW HOW NORTH KOREA BLEW
UPON THE FOUTH OF JULY?

BANGING OUT SEVEN SHORT RANGE MISSILES,
JUST TO LIGHT UP THE SKY!

TAKING IT BACK TO IRAQ,
REALLY OPENED *MY EYES.*
I GUESS
OUR QUEST,
FOR NEW SOURCES OF ENERGY,
WAS NOT MUCH OF A SURPRISE.

BUT WHO ARE WE TO JUDGE
A HOMELAND SO AFFLICTED BY *DRUGS?*

RUNNING UP IN AFGHANISTAN,
WHERE ALL THOSE POPPY SEEDS BUD.

EMBRACING SOME THUGS OUT TO MUG,
WITH A KISS AND HUG.

JUST WATCH THEM STRAIGHT-JACKET ME UP,
THROW ME IN CELL LIKE A BUG.

FLAG FULL OF STRIPES,
LET'S SPARK THE HYPE!
RID OUR WORLD OF THE STRIFE.

SOMEHOW TAKE BACK WHAT IS OURS,
FROM THOSE SNEAKS IN THE NIGHT.

SEVEN HUNDRED EIGHTY-SEVEN BILLION,
WAS SHELLED OUT BY HUNDREDS OF MILLIONS.

BUT I'VE YET TO SEE A DOLLAR
WITH MY BILLS PILING TO THE CEILING.

DOWN SLOPES WE FEEL IT,
IN OFF SHORE DRILLINGS,
GLOBAL WARMING,
HOT OFF THE *SKILLET.*

THOSE GREEN HOUSE,
GASES UP AND RISING,
THOSE CUTS ON THAT ICE,
MAKE A KILLING.

WERE BOMBING BUILDINGS,
STARVING CHILDREN,
EMOTIONALLY TORN IN OUR SPIRIT.

THIS HERE IS MENTALLY OVERWHELMING,
I KNOW YOU PHYSICALLY FEEL IT.

RECESSION BOOMING!
PROJECTING RUMORS,
PROPAGANDA SPARKS US NO SOOTHING.

ARE YOU READY FOR THE COMING ELECTION,
TO PLACE MORE FREEZE ON YOUR MOVEMENT?

JUST GET UP AND DO IT!
GET OUT YOUR BLUE PRINT,
HOLDUP THE WORLD WHILE YOU'RE MOVING.

EXPLORE THE CONTENTS OF YOUR MIND,
BECAUSE THERE IS, NOTHING LEFT BUT CONFUSION.

From King to Kingpin

THEY STRAYED US AWAY FROM YOUR DREAMS,
BY PROVIDING THE PEOPLE WITH THE MEANS
TO BE FIENDS.

OUR COLLECTION OF HANDS,
FELL OVER TRIPLE BEAMS.

WHILE ROLE MODELS, THAT'S CLAIMED,
ARE IN THE MUSIC STREAM.
COINSIDENTLY SINGING . . . ,
"IT WAS ALL A DREAM"!

BUT REALLY WHAT DOES THAT MEAN?
ARE MY DREAMS TOO FAR FETCHED
TO BE REALITY?
I WAS SO UNFOCUSED,
IT TOOK A WHILE TO SEE.

WONDERING WHY WERE MY TEACHERS PAID
TO LIE TO ME?

INDICATING SOCIETY,
DEALT WITH EQUALITY,
OUTSIDE OF MY WINDOW
WAS ONLY POVERTY.

HEART BROKEN SOULS,
VICTIMS OF ROBBERY.

THESE ECOMINICAL CONDITIONS,
ONLY AROUSED MY SUSPICIONS.
LIKE MOMMY,
WHY WE HAVE NO FOOD IN THE KITCHEN?

FATHER,
"WOMAN",
WHAT THE HELL YOU MEAN THAT YOU SPENT IT!

HIS TRAIN WAS BOARDING TRACKS,
BUT HIS TOKENS WERE MISSING.

NOW UNCLE SAM,
WHAT THE HELL YOU MEAN YOU WERE FISHING!

WITH NETS SUSTAINING HOLD
OF LARGE QUANTITIES OF SHIPMENTS.

NOW TAKE THIS GUN,
YOU BETTER GO,
HANDLE YOUR BUSINESS.

NOW, LISTEN SON,
YOU'RE ONLY GOING WIND UP IN PRISON.

YOU ACHIEVED TO SEND YOUR MESSAGE,
BUT I THINK THAT WE MISSED IT.

NOW, MARTIN LUTHER HIT'EM
WITH A DOSE OF THE TRUTH.

OF HOW WE SHOULD ALL COME TOGETHER,
TAKE THIS HATE OUT OUR FUTURE.

The Omen

HE WAS HIS OWN BEST KEPT *SECRET.*

A SPAWN FROM THE *GATES OF HELL!*

HIS PERCEPTION HAD STRONGLY SHOWN HIM.

WHAT NOBODY WOULD YET TO TELL.

WHERE HE IS GOING,
IT IS AS DEEP AS *THEE ABYSS.*

WHAT HE IS SHOWING,
IS THE MARK OF 666?

NO WAY OF TELLING,
YOU OR I,
WHERE HE IS GOING TO RESIDE.
SO STOP . . .

AND BE HONEST WITH YOURSELF.
FOR A MINUTE BECAUSE . . .

YOU DON'T REALLY WANNA KNOW HIS NAME,
BOXED IN,
SHOT,
CUT,
MIXED UP,
BURNING IN FLAMES!

WITH THEM THUGS OUT,
WAITING TO CLAIM.

SMASHING HEADS OUT,
JUST FOR CONTESTING HIS GAIN.

YOU DON'T REALLY WANNA,
BALL IN THIS QUARTER.

KNOWING PO-PO
RECORDED THOSE ORDERS,
BUMPING BUD FROM UP
OUT OF THE WATER.

SNATCHING COKE ROCKED UP,
DISTRIBUTED TO CALLERS.

YOU DON'T REALLY WANNA,
OPEN HIS EYES,
BECAUSE ON THE WAKE UP,
YOUR REPUTATION JUST DIES.
HE'S MASHING OUT,
THOSE SAMPLING PIES,
AND FIENDS *STACK BACK UP,*
IN THEIR RETURN TO MAKE BUYS.

YOU DON'T REALLY WANNA,
RESORT TO THOSE SKILLS.
KIDNAPPING CATS UP,
UNLEASHING DOGS,
CHARGING TO KILL.
EMPTYING MAGS OUT,
SPARKING A PHIL.
SENDING DEE-TEES AROUND,
ABOUT MARKETING DEALS.

WHO WOULD EVER WANNA,
WALK IN HIS SHOES.
ALL SMOKED OUT,
DROPPING THOSE JEWELS.
HITTING PAWN SHOPS,
PLOTTING WITH FOOLS.
MASKING CAPERS,

TAKING PAPER,
WITH THOSE BURGLARY MOVES.

YOU DON'T REALLY WANNA,
FEEL THAT FEAR,
STRAPPED INTO AN ELECTRICAL CHAIR,
WITH CURRENTS BEAMING DIAMETRICAL SPHERES.
MINDS BLOWING, SOULS SHOWING
ANOTHER DEADED CAREER.

YOU DON'T REALLY WANT HIM,
TO DRINK THAT LIQUOR.
TICK HER OFF
BY PROVIDING A PICTURE.
MAKE HER THINK ABOUT
WHY SHE WAS WITH YOU.
BLOW HER TOP OFF,
TAKE YOUR WIFE FROM YOU MISTER.

YOU DON'T REALLY WANNA,
MASK HIS FACE.
MIND FLOWING
LIKE A BASKET CASE.
HEART PUMPING
AT A RAPID PACE.
CHOKED UP,
DRIP STUCK,
LEAVING YOU WITH AN AFTERTASTE.

HE DIDN'T REALLY WANNA,
HEAR THAT VERSE.
THROWING HOLY WATER
ON HIS DIABOLICAL CURSE.
EXORCISM BY
THE CATHOLICAL CHURCH.

POSSESSION LOST.
HE SPENT OFF
AND JUMPED BACK IN THE DIRT.

Fight Terrorism

UNDER THE OCEAN,
THEY EXPLODE THEIR CARGO.
EARTHQUAKE AND TSUNAMIS,
THEIR MOTTO.

FLOODING THE STREETS WITH CHOKES AND STRONG
HOLDS.
BREAKING UP PLATES WITH *DIABLO.*

BLOODY RIVERS, TUMBLING TOWERS,
NUCLEAR PLANTS WITHOUT POWER.

CONVERTING SEEDS TO POWDER,
CROPPING UP ACRES THAT SOUR.

THEY LIKE TO SHAKE UP THOSE IN POWER.
WATCH THEM RUN LIKE THEY'RE COWARDS.

YOU TUBE THEIR FINAL HOURS.
TOSS'EM IN THE GRAVE WITH NO FLOWERS.
DAY BY DAY,
THEY BLOW THEM TORCHES,
DRAWING ASHES FROM CORPSES.

PERISHING OPPOSING FORCES,
PROMOTING WIDOWS AND ORPHANS.

THEY PULL-UP IN THOSE BULLET PROOF CARAVANS,
DROPPING OFF THOSE BROADS
FROM AFGHANISTAN.
WHO OPT
TO RUN UP

IN YOUR STOREFRONT.
BLOW OUT THE BACK DOORS
OF YOUR ESTABLISHMENT.

THEIR TERROR CAMP IS SHIFTING,
PUSHING WEIGHT LIKE A *CATTLE RANCH.*

THEIR CHARLIE ANGELS
HOLD THEM STAKE OUTS,
SNATCHING PLATES FROM THE TALIBAN.

SPITTING THAT LAVA!

THEY QUICK TO THROW A TWIST
IN THE DRAMA,
AND THEY'LL RECRUIT YOUR BABY MAMAS,
IF YOU FALL OUT OF LINE UP.

RESURRECTING OSAMA!

WE UP AGAINST THOSE SUICIDE BOMBERS.
WATCH FIRE RAIN ON OUR IMPALA.
WATCH THEM *POP THE CLUTCH WITH OBAMA.*

DETONATE THAT MOVADO!

ELEVATE THE STREETS OF CHICAGO,
RELEASING THE CONSTRAINTS OF THOSE EMBARGOS,
BY RAISING GRAVE SIGHTS AND SIDEWALKS.

WE'RE UP AGAINST A MILITIA
OF MALICIOUS,
VICIOUS KILLERS,
RIPPING THE COAST UP WITH IMPULSIVE,
ATROCIOUS EXPLOSIONS,
FEROCIOUSLY WAKING,
AND SHAKING UP OUR HABITAT.

Primetime

BUTTER,

ONE OF THE HUMBLEST OF BROTHERS.

WOULD ALWAYS WALK IN PEACE,
REMAINING MINDFUL OF OTHERS.

A MOTORIST,
CERTIFIED PHLEBOTOMIST,
POSSESSED BY AUTO RETAIL,
TRANSFORMED INTO OPTIMUS.

IMMORTALIST,
FAR FROM A CHAUVENIST.

HIS CHILDREN ALWAYS MISSED HIM,
BUT THEY NEVER WERE FATHERLESS.

THE NOBLEST,
MARRIED THE WOMAN
WHO *BORE HIS KIDS.*

THE EVIDENCE ONLY SHOWED
THAT HE COVERED THE ROAD IN SKIDS.

CONVICTING HIM.

VINDICATION,
UPLIFTED HIM.

PEELING OFF AS THE SUNSET,
IS HOW I REMEMBERED HIM?

Stuck in the Past

YOU WILL NEVER BE ABLE TO SEE,
WHO I AM TODAY,
BECAUSE YOU'RE FOCUS
LACKS THE ABILITY TO SEE
BEYOND MY YESTER YEARS.

YOU WILL NEVER KNOW,
WHAT MOVES MY HEART,
BECAUSE YOUR SENSE OF TOUCH
WILL NEVER FEEL ANYTHING
BEYOND THE BEAT OF IT'S GENERAL PULSE.

YOU WILL NEVER BE MOVED,
BY THE SOUND OF MY VOICE,
BECAUSE YOUR MIND WILL REMAIN
STAGNATED IN A PARALYZED STATE,
INCAPABLE OF TAKING HEED
TO THE DIRECTION OF MY MESSAGE.

YOU WILL NEVER REMOLD
A POSITIVE CHANGE FOR YOURSELF,
BECAUSE YOUR SOUL CRIES OUT,
FOR SOCIAL ACCEPTANCE,
OF THOSE WHO LIVE IN THE NEGATIVE.

AM I HYPOCRITE
FOR USING THE WORD "NEVER"?

I BELIEVE SO.

Self-Introspection

ALL IS POSSIBLE,
WHEN ONE TRULY DECIDES
TO MAKE A CHANGE,
BUT IF YOU DON'T DECIDE TO DO IT TODAY,
THEN YOU MAY NEVER WILL.

YOU MAY TURN TO TAKE A SECOND GLANCE,
OF THE REFLECTION OF MY YESTER YEARS,
AND INSTEAD OF FINDING A DEPICTION
OF MY OLD SELF,
YOU MAY FIND A REFLECTION
OF YOUR TRUE SELF.

Jewels of a Conspiracy

DECEPTIVELY,
SOME CONJURE THE IDEAS
OF PROJECTING A MIND GAME.

THE RELEVANCY SIGNIFIED,
BECAUSE OF THE VIEWING BEHIND FRAMES.

PAINTING COLORFUL PICTURES,
WHILE THEY SCHEME.

IMPOLITE SOCIAL DISORDERS
AREN'T ALWAYS WHAT THEY SEEM.

DISPOSITIONS,
CRIPPLE THEIR FATE,
DISSAPATING ATTRACTION,
TALLYING OFF,
SUMMING UP THE SCORES
WITH DISSATISFACTION.

SPAWNING
DIABOLICAL IMPLANTATIONS
AND FIXATIONS.

MOMENTOUSLY,
TOTALLY PRECIOUS,
NEVERTHELESS,
THEIR TIME WAS SPENT WASTED.

Body Language

TREMBLES THAT FILL THE INNER SPIRIT
ARE OVERCOME BY
INTERNAL ENERGY MANIFESTING
MUTUAL STIMULATIONS,
SHAKING AND AWAKENING,
CONSCIOUS THOUGHTS SCRAMBLING
THROUGH PAINTED PICTURES OF MEMORIES,
CONTROLLED BY ONES FRAME OF MIND.

HABITUAL PREMEDITIATIONS,
BORE RAMIFICATIONS
DUE TO FIXATIONS IGNITED BY THE FREE WILL,
OF AN OUT STRETCHED HAND TO RETRIEVE
A GLASS OF WINE.

GATHERINGS BREAK FROM PEACEFUL CONVERSATIONS,
ERUPTING INTO ARGUMENTATION,
DRIVEN BY UNBALANCED MANNERISMS EXPRESSED,
BECAUSE OF HIS GESTURE TO SPAWN A WINK OF AN EYE.

JEALOUS FLASHES,
STRIKE BEHIND EYELASHES,
WITNESSING THE BAT OF HIS WIFE'S EYE
IN REPLY.

The Power of Propaganda

EXPOSED PROJECTIONS,
SHATTERED MIRRORS LEAVING,
DEPICTIONS OF PAST REFLECTIONS.
GRASPING AHOLD
OF SUBCONSCIOUS THOUGHTS.

WARPING THEIR MINDS THROUGH TUNNELED VISIONS,
WHICH INFURIATED AND AGGRAVATED
THE INNER CORE OF ONE LOST SOUL.

BROKEN GLASS COLLECTIVELY SHOWCASED
EVERY MOMENT YET TO UNFOLD.

VISUALIZING,
BASHING GAVELS,
AS THE REQUEST OF ORDER FILLS A COURT.

A SCHOOL TEACHER CROSSED,
LAYED DOWN BY HAMMERS,
ROSE PROTESTERS FOR THE CULPRIT SOUGHT.

COPS GREW WICKED,
IN RESPONSE TO PICKETS,
CONTESTING FOR THEIR THRILLER
TO BE PRODUCED IN COURT.

THE POST WROTE GIMMICKS
FOR THEIR MODERN LYNCHING,
INSURING A CONVICTION
OF THE PERP THEY THOUGHT.

PERVERSED RENDITIONS,
PUT HIM AWAY IN PRISON,
DISTRAUGHT
BY A SYSTEM THAT WAS CORRUPT AND BOUGHT.

A LIFE OF BIDDING
IS WHAT THEY'D GIVEN,
TO THAT INNOCENT MAN THEY'D FAULT.
NOW REALIZING,
TEARING EYES SHED
OVER THE KISS OF *UNSPOKEN THOUGHTS.*

BLACK ROSE POSED,
CRUSH TUX PROVIDED AT THE EXPENSE
OF *A JURIES' LOSS.*

Roses Left on Tables

WHILE I ABSORB
THE SMELL OF YOU PRETTY FLOWER,
I THINK I'LL HAVE A MARTINI.

SHE TAKES FLIGHT,
CUTTING CURBS,
HER EYES SLANTED DREAMY.

HER BODY WAS RIGHT DISPLAYING,
CURVES I THOUGHT I WAS DREAMING.

EXCUSE ME, MS. NATIVE OF THE BRONX,
COULD YOU PROVIDE ME WITH A BETTER SEATING?

HER NAILS WERE RIGHT,
CAUSING SLURRS
AS WE BEGAN SPEAKING.

THOSE STARES THAT NIGHT,
CAUSED SOME STIRS
BODY FLUIDS BEGAN LEAKING.

HEY THERE, MS. MID-FORTY,
BEHIND CLOSE DOORS
ARE YOU NAUGHTY?

SHE SMILED BACK,
MAKING SURE THAT OUR TALK
WAS IN SECRET.

WHAT WE SHARED THAT NIGHT,
CAUSED A PURR,
SHE BEDDED A KEEPER.

HEY THERE, LITTLE CUTIE,
NOW THAT I'M IN YOUR GATED COMMUNITY,
WOULD YOU PROVIDE ME WITH IMMUNITY?

WE LAYED ALL NIGHT,
TOSSED AND TURNED,
AS I THRUST THROUGH HER DEEPER.

SHE WHISPERED
"OOH DADDY" IN THE AIR
AS I POKED OUT AND REACHED HER.

HEY THERE, LIL' NIGHTY WAITRESS,
CAN I HOLLAR AT YOU ON YOUR DAY SHIFT?

SOMETHING MISSING,
WAS NOW IN HER LIFE,
AS I CONTINUED TO SINK IN.

WE PLAYED ALL DAY,
WORKED ALL NIGHT,
OUR LOVE LIFE WAS PEAKING.

Offspring

BREATH IS FLOWN BETWEEN TWO INDIVIDUALS
AS THOUGH THEY WERE BREATHING AS ONE.

STIMULATION WAS STEADILY INCREASING,
ALTHOUGH THEIR PERFORMANCE HAD ONLY BEGUN.

HER INSIDES WERE BEGGING FOR ATTENTION,
AS THOUGH SHE WANTED THEM TOUCHED.

WHICH FORCED THE CHANGE
OF BOTH OF THEIR POSITION,
AS HE BEGAN TO ENTER AND THRUST

WHAT SEEPED THROUGH HIS AND HER BODY,
CAN ONLY BE DESCRIBED AS A RUSH.

EXPLOSIONS HAD BEGUN TO OCCUR INTERNALLY,
AS BOTH OF THEM PROCEEDED TO BUST.

MILLIONS OF TELESCOPICAL CELLS,
SWAM UP HER CANAL LIKE A FISH.

THE ESSENCE OF SUCH A PERFORMANCE
HAD ONLY DERIVED FROM HIS AND HER BLISS.

ALTHOUGH THEIR RACE TOGETHER,
STARTED OFF BY THE SHOT OF A GUN.

THERE WOULD BE NO SECOND OR THIRD PLACE WINNERS,
THERE ONLY STOOD A PRIZE FOR ONE.

WITH THAT SPECIAL ENGAGEMENT,
WHICH WAS SOON TO BE PRIVATELY HELD.

THAT SEED BECAME VERY FAMILIAR,
WITH WHAT IS KNOWN AS HER OVUM CELL.

A CONNECTION HAD BEEN MADE,
PRETTY MUCH DUE TO THEIR FAMILIARIZATION.

A NEW COURSE OF ACTION WAS NOW TAKING PLACE,
OTHERWISE KNOWN AS FERTILIZATION.

TWENTY-ONE DAYS HAD PASSED,
ALTHOUGH HER STOMACH WOULD YET TO SHOW.

INCUBATING INSIDE OF HER BODY,
WAS NOW KNOWN AS AN EMBRYO.

TWO AND A HALF MONTHS GONE BY,
AS SHE WOULD SCARF DOWN UNUSUAL FOODS TO FEED IT.

THE EMBRYO HAD NOW SHIFTED AND CHANGED,
TOOK ON THE FORM OF A FETUS.

ONE HUNDRED-EIGHTY DAYS LATER,
EXHAUSTED FROM THE STRAIN TO ENDURE,
HIS FIRST BREATH OF LIFE.

SURGEONS SWIFTLY PERFORMED
THEIR FINAL PROCEDURE,
CONGRATULATING THAT HUSBAND AND WIFE.

CONGRATULATIONS!

Running a Different Race

AS I SAT BACK THINKING
ABOUT A RHYME TO WRITE.
I WAS A LIL' UPTIGHT
ABOUT WHAT HAPPENED LAST NIGHT,
BETWEEN ME AND MY SHORTY.
WE WAS GOING THROUGH IT!
SHE WAS QUICK TO THROW A FIT,
OVER EVERYTHING I DID!
I NEVER REALIZED HER FAMILY,
NEVER APPROVED OF THE KID.

AND I BEGAN TO QUESTION WHY
WE NEVER SLID TO HER CRIB.
BUT FEELINGS QUICKLY CHANGED
WHEN SHE BEGAN TO ADMIT,
SAYING,
"DAMIEN,
YOU DON'T EVEN KNOW THE HALF OF IT.
THAT MY PARENTS ARE REALLY MOVING
ON SOME RACIST SHIT.
THEY REALLY WANT
NO PARTS OF OUR RELATIONSHIP!"

THAT'S WHEN OUR HEARTS CAVED IN,
WE LEANED FORWARD FOR A KISS,
AND I KNEW RIGHT FROM THEN
SHE WOULD BE THE ONE I MISSED.

MR. AND MRS. GENNA,
IT'S FUNNY
HOW TIMES HAVE CHANGED,
AND RACISM PERSIST TO EXIST TODAY.

YOU WOULD THINK THOSE THOUGHTS OF HATE,
WOULD HAVE BEEN GONE AND BURIED.
BUT HOW WILL WE EVER
GET ALONG WITH EACH OTHER,
IF WE NEVER REALLY REACHED OUT
AND EMBRACED ONE ANOTHER?
IT'S TIME TO KILL THE HATE.
MOVE ON,
CONGRATULATE.
REGARDLESS OF OUR ETHINICITY
OR WHERE WE COME FROM,
WE ARE ALL GOD'S CHILDREN.

"PEACE."

Love at First Sight

GIRL,
YOUR ATTRACTION,
IS SO DISTRACTING,
IT HAS MY SOUL CRYING OUT FOR YOU.

YOU'RE SO PATIENT,
I'M SO ANXIOUS,
MY HEART HAS FALLEN IN LOVE TOO SOON.

COME HERE BABY,
MY SWEET LADY,
NO NEED TO WORRY,
CAUSE I'LL TREAT YOU RIGHT.

JUST RELAX
AND WORK YOUR MAGIC,
SEND ME CRAWLING
INTO THOSE EYES.

THERE'S NO ESCAPING,
MY SWEET BABY,
OUR HUDDLE
WILL BE SO TIGHT.

SLOW TRACTION,
TENDER ACTION,
WE WILL CUDDLE
ALL THROUGH THE NIGHT.

OUR ATTACHMENT,
REACHING AND GRASPING,
YES, OUR LOVING
WILL BE SO RIGHT.

IT'S SO CRAZY,
I'LL BE THINKING,
HOW FAR I'VE FALLEN
INTO YOUR EYES.

YOUR ATTRACTION,
IT'S SO DISTRACTING,
IT HAS MY SOUL CRYING OUT FOR YOU.

IT'S SO CRAZY,
I'LL BE THINKING
HOW I HAVE FALLEN
IN LOVE WITH YOU.

WE ARE MAXING,
IT IS MAGIC,
AND I HAVE FALLEN
INTO YOUR EYES.

OH, SWEET BABY,
IT'S SO CRAZY,
HOW I HAVE FALLEN
IN LOVE WITH YOU.

Crime Waves

WHAT WAS HIS CRIME?

WHAT WAS THE DESIRED RESULT?

WHAT ACTUALLY HAPPENED?

WHAT WAS AFFECTING HIS THOUGHTS?

WAS IT THE HIGH
OR THE LOVE FOR THE FUNDS?

PERHAPS,
IT WAS THE CONNECTIONS
THAT HE MADE WITH SOMEONE.

WHAT WAS HIS CRIME?

A Pretty Blue Sea

IN THE REFLECTIONS OF THE MIRRORS OF HER SOUL,
SHE RELINQUISHED CONTROL.
UNVEILING THE BEAUTY
OF HER PRECIOUS BLUE SEA.

HE STOOD AT HER SHORE,
ENJOYING THE VIEW OF IT ALL.
PRE-EMPTIVELY DRAWN
INTO THE POINT OF HIS KNEES.

SLOWLY WERE RIPPLES
AS COLD HARDENED HER NIPPLES.
FINDING ROSE PETALS
ON THE STREAKS OF HER SURFACE.

HE MOTIONED TO SWIM,
WITH MUSCLE SWOLLEN LIMB
AND HEAT AROSE LIKE THAT OF A FURNACE.

FOUND AFLOAT,
DEEP IN A STROKE,
HER CURRENT BEGUN
TO GUIDE HIS DIRECTION.

HER MOTION
GREW FULL AND INTENSE.

HIS LAGGING
WAS THE ONLY EXCEPTION.

WITH MUSCLE LIMBS BURNING
AND KNEES SLOWLY BENDING,
ABOUT ON THE VERGE OF A BUCKLE.

A CLEARING OF HIS THROAT,
LEFT A PASSAGE OF AIR,
ONLY HEARD WAS THE SOUND OF HER CHUCKLE.

ENDURANCE ASSISTED HIS PERSISTANCE,
SLOWLY DRIFTING A DISTANCE,
FINDING HIMSELF DEEPER IN HER WATERS.

CLOTHING DRENCHED,
PUSHED TO THE SIDE,
SINKING HIM SLOWLY
AS DEEP AS A QUARTER.

GASPING FOR AIR,
AS BUBBLES AROSE,
RELEASED FROM THE CORE OF HIS LUNGS.

HE BEGAN *SWIMMING* AND *STROKING,*
AS FAST AS HE COULD,
IT WAS HER FEELING OF HIM BEING STRUNG.

HIS LIPS FINALLY,
BROKE THROUGH HER SURFACE.

HER MOISTURE,
SLOWLY SOAKENED HIS TONGUE.

HER CURRENT LAPPED,
AT THE BACK OF HIS HEAD,
HER WAVES WERE DESTINED TO COME.

HE MUSTERED HIS STRENGTH,
SWAM THROUGH PRETTY BLUE,
CATCHING EACH ONE BY ONE.

HE WASHED ASHORE,
SWOLLEN LIMBS HIT LAND,
AND PRETTY BLUE
WAS THE CAUSE OF HIS PLUNGE.

Wet Dreams

PASSIVELY,
HER EYES AWAKENS
MY INNER MOST DESIRES.
AS I'M HYPNOTICALLY,
MESMERIZED
WITHIN THE COMFORT ZONE OF THIS DREAM.

WITH A MOTION,
THAT IS SEDUCTIVELY WITH PRECISION,
SHE ENHANCES WITHIN MY VISION,
DISPLAYING WHAT IS INTRICATELY,
DESIGNED FOR A QUEEN

RAPIDLY EXPOSED,
AT A STARE,
WE ENGULF IN ONE AIR SWIMMING
AT THE FOLD OF HER TONGUE AND ITS RING.

WE PROGRESS,
AT OUR CARESS,
AS MY NAME BEATS HER CHEST,
MIRRORS REFLECT A POLE AT HER SEAMS.

AS TEMPERATURE GROWS HEATED.
SHE RE-ITERATES WHATS NEEDED.
RAPTURE DEFINES THE FORCE OF MY SPANK.

A SECTION OF MANE,
BECOMES PULLED.
A PALM FILLS HER ORIFICE,
HER BREATH IN HER LUNGS BECOMES TANKED.

OUR CLASH IN OPPOSITION,
RE-ENFORCES OUR CONDITION,
A MOMENT PUTS A SHUT IN HER EYES.

HER RESPIRATION IS RESTORED!
MY LIDS NOW PEEL OVER!
SHE LEFT WITHOUT EVEN SAYING GOODBYE.

WET DREAMS.

Pulsate

HER EYES CRAWLED,
FROM BEHIND BLINDS,
AS SHE ABSORBED
THE TOUCH OF HIM.
SLOWLY MOTIONING
HIS FINGERTIPS DOWNWARD,
TOWARDS HER THIGHS.

THEIR STIMULATION ROSE HIGH!
SENSATIONS GRAVITATEDLY VIBRATED,
ALONG WITH THE BEAT OF HER PULSE.
PUMPING AND POUNDING,
SLOWLY FROM HIS LOVE INDUCING,
PACK-PUNCHING RUM.

MET UPON EXTRACT,
IN FULL CONTACT,
WERE THEIR TONGUES.

FALLING TO THE DEPTH OF A LUNGE,
HIS HANDS CREPT PAST HER THONGS,
ONLY TO STOP,
SHORT OF HER BUNG.

SHE WAS WET!
IT WAS ON!

SKULL AND BONE TORE
WITHIN HER WALLS.
SHE SOAKED HIS HEAD,
HE STAINED HER DRAWS.

THE NEIGHBORS WATCHED!
THE CURTAINS WERE DRAWN!

THEY HEARD HER MOAN
AND HUMMED HER SONG.

MRS. KEYES' *"A WOMAN WORTH"*.

Breaking Her In

HUNG OF HER SEAMS,
LIES TWO KEYS
BEING SWUNG BACK AND FORTH.

THERE SWINGING
ROSE TO TONES ABOVE SILENCE,
AS THEY JUMPED AND JERKED,
BY THE MEANS
OF HER FLESH AND CLOTH.

IN A COLLECTIVE MOTION,
OF OBTAINING ONE,
WITH HER LOTIONED FINGERTIPS.

SHE CHOICEFULLY SELECTED A KEY,
HOLDING IT WITHIN
THE CONFINEMENT OF HER FIST.

ADJUSTING THE KEY WITHIN HER HAND,
RAISING HER LEGS TO TWO SETS OF STAIRS.

SHE MOTIONED THE KEY TO A HOLE,
WHICH WOULD SUCCUMB TO NO AVAIL.

ASSISTING HER WITH HER TASK
WAS A WARM AND DELICATE HAND.

WIGGLING IT SIDE TO SIDE
WAS A BROWN EYED HUNCHBACK MAN.

DISTRAUGHT AND FRUSTRATED,
NOTICING HER NEIGHBOR,
WHO CAUGHT A GLIMPSE.

SHE RETRIEVED THE KEY FROM HIS HAND
AND PLACED IT BETWEEN HER LIPS.

WITH THE MOTION OF HER UPPER TORSO,
LEANING BACK AND FORTH.

THE KEY BRUSHED AGAINST HER TEETH,
WHILE HE HUNCHED AND SPLIT HER DOOR.

*GRIPPING AT ITS KNOB,
IN, WHICH SLOWLY BEGAN TO FLINCH.*

SHE RELEASED THE KEY FROM HER MOUTH,
APPARENTLY NEEDING TO SPIT.

WITH A SECOND BODY MOTION BEGINNING
TO ROCK AGAINST HER DOOR.

SHE CURVED AND BENT,
A SECOND KEY,
WHICH WAS THROWN AGAINST HER WALL.

AS HIS HANDS WAS BEGINNING
TO CARESS HER SHOULDERS,
PROVIDING SOME MEANINGFUL SUPPORTIVE ASSISTANCE.

SHE LOOKED BACK,
ONLY TO WITNESS,
A HARDENED FACIAL DISPOSITION.

FEELING THE WARMTH IN THEIR GESTURES,
WHILE THEIR BROWN EYES SUNK WITHIN HER GROOVE.

THEY RELEASED THE TOOLS FROM THEIR BELTS
KNOWING EXACTLY WHAT TO DO.

ONE HAMMERED HER FRONT DOOR,
WHILE THE OTHER,
JIMMIED HIS WAY THROUGH THE BACK.

ONE BANGING TO INDUCE A HOLE,
THE OTHER, EASING HIS WAY
THROUGH A CRACK.

BOTH DOORS OPENED SIMULTANIOUSLY,
AS THOUGH HER HOUSE
WAS UNDER ATTACK.

IN HER RELIEF,
OF THEE ACCOMPLISHMENT
ACHIEVED IN BOTH OF THEIR MISSIONS.

SHE WELCOMED THE TWO
TO SOMETHING TO EAT,
POLISHING
THE BOTH OF THEIR HEADS GLISTENING.

Sinking Ships

EXERCISING WITHIN,
KNOWN FORBIDDEN DESIRES.
SHE SEDUCES ME WITH HER GLANCE.
PROMOTING FLUIDS TO MOVE,
THROUGHOUT MY BODY ERUPTING
INTO THE WELCOMED SENSATIONS
OF HER TALENTED INSTRUMENT.
SWIRLING AND LAPPING,
OVER WAVES THAT CLASHED AGAINST
THE SHORES OF A PRETTY BLUE SEA.

WEAKENING BOTH OF MY KNEES!

CAPITIVATED
IN HER WARM RESPONSE.
THAT PULSATED AND LEVITATED
WITH MOTIONING PALMS.
THAT SLOWLY BEAT UPON DRUMS.
THAT MYSTIFIED THE AIR,
LIKE JAZZ, BLUES, AND FUNK.

A SHIP'S HORN HAD BLOWN QUICKLY!
THE DOME WILLINGLY REMAINED PUMPED!

BENT AT HER HIPS,
CLOSE TO ABANDONING SHIP.
SHE TIGHTENED HER LIPS
AND RELEASED FROM HER GRIP.

THE WIT
OF HER HEALTHY HEAD PLAY
WAS SICK!

Infidelity

HIS VISION
HAS BEEN BLURRED,
BY THE BUBBLES INCREASING
WITHIN HER PUPILS.

HIS HEART
HAS INCREASED IN PACE
AND HIS MOOD
IS NO LONGER SUBTLE.

FRUSTRATION
FILLS HIS EMOTIONS,
WISHING IT WERE ALL AN ILLUSION.

BUT HIS EYES HAVE NEVER LIED,
SO, HE'S IN A STATE OF CONFUSION.

HE KNOWS
SECRETS REMAINED IN CLOSETS,
SHUT AND FORBIDDEN.

BUT HOW MUCH COULD ONE CLOSET HOLD,
EXACTLY,
HOW MUCH WAS HIDDEN?

WHAT CAUSED SUCH GRIEF
AND DECREASE IN PRODUCTION?

IS THE SIGHT BEFORE HIS EYES,
THE REASON
THEIR MARRIAGE MALFUNCTIONED?

COULD THE TEARS FROM HER EYES
MEND HIS HEART,
PROVIDING THOUSANDS OF STITCHES?

OR WILL HEADLINES
VOICE A COVER STORY
SURROUNDED BY PICTURES?

HISTORY HAS PLAYED IT WORST,
JUST REVIEW IT IN SCRIPTURE.

TO PREVENT SUCH A SITUATION
LEAVING TWO HEARTS FROZEN.

LET ONE LOVE AND DEVOTION,
BE THE ONE TO BE CHOSEN.

ALL THE DECEIVING,
MISLEADING,
AFTER DISCUSSIONS AND PLEADING.

IS CLEARLY UNNECESSARY,
IF HE'S THE ONE YOU ARE NEEDING.

PROTECT HIS EYE SIGHT
AND SECURE ALL CLOSET DOORS.

DON'T ATTEMPT TO BLIND HIS EYES,
WITH THOSE TEARS FOUND IN YOURS.

*HIS VISION
HAS BEEN BLURRED,
BY THE BUBBLES INCREASING
WITHIN HER PUPILS.*

Heaven or Hell

MY SOUL WAS CAUGHT UP
WITHIN THE MIST
OF SPINNING DARK MATTER.

RAYS FROM THE SUN,
WHERE WITHIN MY REACH.
BUT MY GRASP FELL COLD,
DUE TO THE TEMPERATURE
OF AN OVER SHADOWING ECLIPSE.

I WAS IN THE PRESENCE,
OF GOOD AND EVIL'S CLASHING SILOHUETTE.
AS I BECAME PAUSED
IN THE CENTER OF THE UNIVERSE.

I VANISHED WITHIN
THE BLINK OF AN EYE!

STAGNATED IN TIME!

TRANSPORTING IN
AND DISCHARGING OUT
OF A BLACK HOLE,
MY SOUL WAS PUSHED
THROUGH A BLAZING FIRE.

WHILE I TRAVELED THROUGH IT,
I REMEMBERED WHEN.

I FELT VICTIM TO TEMPTATION,
INSTEAD OF PRAYING TO JESUS.

DEMONIC POSSESSORS,
SWOOPED IN AND OUT OF MY SUBCONSCIOUS.

HOOTING,
HOLLERING,
AND SCREAMING!

BLOOD AND TEARS FILLED MY EYES,
RELEASING THOSE DEVILISH SECRETS.
MY SOUL JUST LEFT ME COLD
AND TOOK A LEAP OFF THE DEEP END.

(CHORUS)
"IT'S NOT EVERYDAY
THAT GOOD AND EVIL GOES TO WAR OVER ME.
DROPPING THROUGH TUNNELS,
FIRE BURNING AT TEN THOUSAND DEGREES.
DEATH CLOSED MY EYES,
MY SOUL AWAITS IN FULL OF WONDER TO SEE.
IF EITHER, HEAVEN OR HELL,
WHERE I WAS DESTINED TO BE."

WHILE TERRY AND REBECCA,
SECURED THE SECTOR,
SEDATING HANNIBAL LECTOR.

ANN AND MARG,
HAD MADE THEIR ROUNDS,
PERFORMING GENERAL CHECK UPS.

ONE SICK PATIENT,
WHO SAT WITH JASON,
CLICKING BACK AND FORTH STATIONS.

HAD TURNED AND BEGUN TO CONFESS,
ABOUT THE LIFE HE SPENT WASTED.

HE CHEERED
AND BEGUN HIS STORY,
WITH GUNS BLAZING IN GLORY.

WENT TALLY HO AGAINST AL-QAEDA,
BECAME ADDICTED TO MORPHINE.

RODE OFF ENDORPHINS,
CARRIED COFFINS,
ILLEGALLY ADOPTED AN ORPHAN.

WAS NOT EMOTIONALLY
OR MENTALLY PREPARED,
FOR HIS WIFE'S DIVORCE AND ABORTION.

HIS MISERY ONLY EXCEEDED,
CATCHING SEVERAL DISEASES,
AND WITH A MEDICAL FORMAL DISCHARGE,
HE WAS BACK AT HOME WEEZING.

LAYED UP JUST RECENT,
IN A PRECINT,
FOR SOME ACT OF MALFEASANCE.

HIS CONDITION
WAS NOW POST MORTEM,
THE INNER BEAST WAS UNLEASHING.

(CHORUS)
"IT'S NOT EVERYDAY
THAT GOOD AND EVIL GOES TO WAR OVER ME.
DROPPING THROUGH TUNNELS,
FIRE BURNING AT TEN THOUSAND DEGREES.
DEATH CLOSED MY EYES,
MY SOUL AWAITS IN FULL OF WONDER TO SEE.
IF EITHER, HEAVEN OR HELL,
WHERE I WAS DESTINED TO BE."

WHILE HOSPICE JASON
SHOOK THE BUILDING,
QUOTING BIBLICAL SCRIPTURE.

ANGELS OF DEATH,
SPUN WIND AROUND HIM,
RIPPING THE FLOOR
OUT THE PICTURE.

ALL FOUR WALLS
WERE ENGULFED IN FIRE.
GOD VOICE SPOKE
IN A WHISPER,
SAYING
*"DON'T YOU WORRY ABOUT A THING
BECAUSE I'M COMING TO GET CHA'.*

(CHORUS)
*"IT'S NOT EVERYDAY
THAT GOOD AND EVIL GOES TO WAR OVER ME.
DROPPING THROUGH TUNNELS,
FIRE BURNING AT TEN THOUSAND DEGREES.
DEATH CLOSED MY EYES,
MY SOUL AWAITS IN FULL OF WONDER TO SEE.
IF EITHER, HEAVEN OR HELL,
WHERE I WAS DESTINED TO BE."*

WHILE SEVERAL DEMON SPIRITS
BEGAN EXPLODING AROUND 'EM.

GOD'S ANGELS SECURED THE AREA,
WHERE FIRE ATTEMPTED TO DROWN HIM.

HIS SOUL BEGAN TRANSCENDING
WITH ALL THOSE ANGELS AROUND 'EM.

JASON LOOKED HIM UP,
WHILE OTHERS ATTEMPTED TO DOWN HIM.

(CHORUS)
"IT'S NOT EVERYDAY
THAT GOOD AND EVIL GOES TO WAR OVER ME.
DROPPING THROUGH TUNNELS,
FIRE BURNING AT TEN THOUSAND DEGREES.
DEATH CLOSED MY EYES,
MY SOUL AWAITS IN FULL OF WONDER TO SEE.
IF EITHER, HEAVEN OR HELL,
WHERE I WAS DESTINED TO BE."

"IT'S NOT EVERYDAY
THAT GOOD AND EVIL GOES TO WAR OVER ME.
DROPPING THROUGH TUNNELS,
FIRE BURNING AT TEN THOUSAND DEGREES.
DEATH CLOSED MY EYES,
MY SOUL AWAITS IN FULL OF WONDER TO SEE.
IF EITHER, HEAVEN OR HELL,
WHERE I WAS DESTINED TO BE."

Christmas Gifts

BOTH OFFERED,
AS WELL AS RECEIVED.

YOU MAY FIND MANY SPENDING
COUNTLESS HOURS MAKING
LIST FOR THINGS,
THAT THEY PRAY LAY BURIED
BENEATH A TREE.

TAKE FOR EXAMPLE,
A BOY NAMED JOEY,
WHO BEGGED THAT THIS CHRISTMAS,
HE RECEIVED HIS VERY OWN T.V.

AT AN AGE OF ONLY THIRTEEN,
HE CAN BARELY
SEPARATE A FICTIONAL SCRIPT,
FROM ONE BASED ON REALITY.

LET ALONE EXERCISING
PROFOUND VALUES
WITH A GOOD SENSE OF MORALITY.

WITH THIS NEW RECEIVED SET,
HE'S ALREADY BEGUN TO SUFFER,
FROM A MISBALANCED LIFE STYLE.

THAT IS PREDOMINATELY SPENT
WITH "THRILL SEEKERS",
"GHOST HUNTERS",
"HOG WASH",
AND "CHASE BLUNDERS!"

YOU SEE,
JOEY,
RATHER THAN UTILIZE THE T.V.
TO GATHER VALUABLE INFORMATION,
TO RAISE HIS LEVEL OF WIT.

HE'S ALREADY BEGUN
TO REVAMP HIS LIFE STYLE,
FORMULATING A DYSFUNCTIONAL CHARACTER
FROM OUT THIS T.V. SET.

HOW COULD YOU GROW UPSET?

WHEN THIRTY DAYS EARLIER,
YOU DISREGARDED
ALL OF YOUR LIVING EXPENSES,
LOST ALL YOUR GOOD SENSES,
AND SURPRISED HIM WITH
"MERRY CHRISTMAS,
MERRY CHRISTMAS!"

KNOWING GOOD AND WELL,
A GRAND OPPORTUNITY
HAD BEEN DISMISSED!

RATHER THAN SELECTING
TO HAVE A GOOD TIME.
YOU CHOSE A BAD TIME
FOR POOR SPENDING.

FULLY UNAWARE OF
THE MESSAGE YOU WERE SENDING.
POOR JOEY,
SIMPLY JUST DOESN'T HAVE A CLUE.

THAT MOST OF HIS NEW LEARNED
NEGATIVE BEHAVIOR,
JUST MATERIALIZED FROM OUT OF HIS TUBE.

YOU INWARDLY BEGIN TO PONDER,
"WHAT AM I TO DO?"
"WHAT AMI TO DO?"
I SAY,
"REFLECT CAREFULLY,
ON HOW YOU ARE SPENDING YOUR TIME,
AS A TEACHER ONCE SAID".

"SHARE THE SIGNIFICANCE
OF JESUS BIRTH,
SPEND WITHIN YOUR MEANS INSTEAD".

"CHOOSE A GIFT WISELY,
THAT IS *INCAPABLE* OF PROMOTING BAD INFLUENCE".

"WHEN NEXT CHRISTMAS COMES AROUND,
DON'T YOU LET US HERE
THAT YOU BLEW IT".

CHRISTMAS GIFTS.

DEVOTION,
HEAVILY DWELLS
WITHIN THE HEART
OF ONE GROUP'S SUBCONSCIOUS.

EYES CONNECT,
SIGNIFYING THE WHERE ABOUTS
OF ONE'S SPIRITUAL EXISTENCE.

WORDS FALL TO SILENCE,
FOREFILLING AN EMBRACE
THAT HOLDS RELEVANCE.

REALITY FOUND IN A DREAM,
IS RESTORED TO SHOW
A SIGN OF REMEMBERANCE.

A HURT, TORMENTED SOUL
PLEADS AND BEGS FOR FORGIVENESS.

AN ILLUMINATING SPIRIT,
SUSPENSEFULLY ASCENDS
OUT OF DARKNESS.

CANDLES THAT BURN,
SHOWS AND REFLECT,
A SIGN OF PURENESS.

SPIRITS FILL THE SUBCONSCIOUS
OF AN IMMEDIATE CIRCUMFERENCE.

TURMOIL BUILDS AND SPILLS
FROM THE SOURCE OF ONE'S TRUTHFULNESS.

AN ENGAGEMENT IS HELD
IN ORDER TO UPHOLD
ONE'S SIGNIFICANCE.

A VOW IS MADE
WITH CONFIDENCE OF TRULY MAKING A DIFFERENCE.

BRINGING ONE'S FAMILY TIES BACK
TO THE SOURCE OF ITS ESSENCE.

THERE WILL NEVER BE ANOTHER,
WHO WILL HOLD MY HEART
LIKE YOU.
PLEASE, MOMMY
FORGIVE ME FOR ALL THE PAIN
AND HURT I CAUSED YOU
IN LIFE.

IN LOVING MEMORY OF MY MOTHER,

MRS. COLLETTE TRACY-WALKER

Spiritual Guidance

MISCHANNELED AGGRESSION,
SEEPS THROUGH THE WALLS OF MY OPPRESSION.

CONSTANT PROJECTIONS,
OF A SPIRITUAL REFLECTION,
HAS WARPED IN MY MIND,
CAUSING A PHYSICAL REACTION.

MY EMOTIONS
ARE DEFINED AS DEPRESSING.

A WITH HIDDEN PERCEPTION
OF SUSPENSEFUL DELUSIONS.

CREATED DEBATABLE CONFUSION
AND UNWARRANTED CONCLUSION.

WHAT COULD HAVE SPARKED SUCH A FUSION?

A SHADOW BREAKS INTO MOVEMENT!

WITH NO FURTHER SUPPRESSION,
I BEGIN TO ADDRESS IT
WITH A SOULFUL CONNECTION,
AS IF SOMETHING HAS TAUGHT ME A LESSON.

THE SHADOW ISSUES CORRECTION,
WHICH COMES IN THE FORM OF A BLESSING.

THE SPIRITUAL DIRECTION
HAS COMPLETED THE SESSION.
ONE'S PROFESSION IS FORBIDDEN
TO REVEAL MY CONFESSION.

The Crucifixion

SPIRITUAL REFLECTIONS
OF A SOUL PROVIDING SAVIOR.

BOUND,
TORTURED,
AND SHACKLED,
UNCONTROLLED IN HIS ENDEAVORS.

RIDICULED,
BECAUSE OF HIS MIRACLES,
TORMENTED
BY THEIR BEHAVIOR.

EXPANDED,
A PAIR OF WINGS GUIDED
BY ONE CREATOR.

WINGS FLAP DOWN
TO WITNESS ONE'S PERSECUTION.

SPIKES RIP THROUGH FLESH,
THREE EMERGE IN EXECUTION.

A BODY SECURELY WRAPPED,
HEARTS CAUGHT UP IN A STRUGGLE.

HIS PHYSICAL IS LAID TO REST,
DEEPLY WITH HIDDEN BEHIND RUBBLE.

A STONE IS ROLLED AWAY,
TOO SLOWLY APPROACH WHISPERING.

ASTONISHED,
ARE THEIR EYES,
AS THEIR BREATHING INTENSIFIED.

BEING TOLD WHAT HAD OCCURRED,
AS IF IT WERE ANY OF A SURPRISE.

THE SON OF MAN,
WHO WAS SENT TO BE CRUCIFIED.

RELEASED HIS HOLY SPIRIT
AND JOURNEYED BEYOND THE SKIES.

IT IS NO LONGER,
A WORRY FOR YOU.

NOR IS IT,
A WORRY FOR I.

AS LONG AS OUR SPIRITS
ARE TRULY RICH,
OUR SOULS WILL NEVER DIE.

Now I Lay Me Down to Sleep

MY VISION HAS FROZE
AND ONLY ONE KNOWS,
WHAT I'M LOOKING AT.

SOUNDS OF CONSPIRING VOICES,
DISCUSSING MY DAMNATION,
HAS DISTURBED MY TRAIN OF THOUGHT
AND BROKEN MY CONCENTRATION.

ALONE,
FORSAKEN,
TRAPPED,
AND MISUNDERSTOOD!

THOSE VOICES HAD GROWN LOUDER
AS THEY CIRCLED IN BLACK HOODS.

PIECE BY PIECE,
THEY SEARCHED MY FLESH
TO RETRIEVE MY SOUL.

BUT A HAND FULL OF LAMB
AND A HEART FULL OF GOLD,
IS ALL THEY SEEM TO HOLD.

CURSING WITH OBSCENITIES,
AS THEIR FRUSTRATION GREW STRONGER.

BOUND TO GIVING UP,
AS THEY WISH TO LOOK NO LONGER.

BEAMS OF LIGHT SUDDENLY APPEAR!

TRANSCEDING TO A PLACE,
THEY WISH NOT TO GO NEAR.

BACKS AGAINST THE WALL,
AS THEY HUDDLED IN FEAR.

"WHO SHALL BE DAMNED?"

IS ALL THAT THEY HEAR.

VIBRATIONS AND TREMORS,
SLOWLY OCCUR.

ROCKS AND RUBBLE,
TURNED VISIONS TO BLURR.

LOOKING FOR SALVATION,
YOU MUST TRUST WHERE YOU TURN.

THE *WICKED* AND *UNSAVED,*
WILL ONLY PERISH AND BURN.

TO BE FOUND
IN THE ARMS OF THE ALMIGHTY,
IS SOMETHING THAT'S EARNED.

PLEASE TAKE THIS OCCURRENCE
AS A LESSON THAT'S LEARNED.

AND SEARCH FOR YOUR SAVIOR,
IT COULD SOON BE YOUR TURN!

IT COULD SOON BE YOUR TURN!

IT COULD SOON BE YOUR TURN!

Soundwaves

THE CURRENT MINDS WANNA KNOW,
HOW FAR OFF INTO THE OCEAN,
ONE SHOULD FLOW?

CAN ONE DRIFT
SO DEEP FROM SHORE?
THE SEEDS HE BARES WILL NEVER GROW.

WILL HE CROSS CHANNELS AND STREAMS,
BECOME SPLIT LIKE A BEAN,
SMASHED BY STONE SUNKEN
IN SKELETAL BONE?

DUE TO FREE WILL
THESE QUESTIONS HOLD ANSWERS.
THAT ARE CLEARLY UNFORCERTAIN
AND THOSE WHO REST ASHORE BRAINSTORMING,
ARE LEFT WONDERING.

HOW FAR OFF INTO THE DESERT,
ONE SHOULD GO?

WILL HE ALTER HIS STANCE,
FALL ON LOWER LIMBS AND HANDS,
BECOME UNQUENCHED IN THIRST,
BURIED IN SAND,
AND STILL HAVE THE PLEASURE OF MEETING,
THE MAKER OF MAN?

EYES LOOK OVER PYRAMIDS,
WITNESSING
THE SEVEN WONDERS OF THE WORLD!

THE BODY PROCEEDS
TO ASCEND INTO A KINGDOM
OF NO ORDINARY LAND.

YOU AND I,
MAN AND WOMAN,
MINDS INFINITE,
LIKE SPACE SOULS SURROUNDED BY LAMB.

LET OUR HEARTS GROW BETTER IN TIME,
JUST AS THE WINE,
DELIVERED BY THE SON
FOR WHICH WE STAND.

PLEASE JOIN,
HAND AND HAND,
GIVE APPLAUSE
TO OUR SAVIOR,
AS WELL AS HIS PLAN.

Days of Lent

IMPULSES,
CRIPPLE MY MIND STATE,
AS I GRAVITATE
TOWARDS REFORM.

MY BEHAVIOR,
DEVIATES AND ELEVATES
FROM THE NORM.

THE MOMENT,
PERPETUATES,
STIMULATING A SPAWN.

MY HEART
BEGINS TO CRY OUT,
BRING THE RUCKUS,
IT'S ON!

"A YO, MIKE
SEND ME THE WORD OUT,
FILL THE SPEAKERS WITH TONES!"

OL LE, SACA LAS CHICAS,
BECAUSE THIS SSSSHHHH . . . . IS A BOMB!

A-YO, LANCE,
I'M ABOUT TO GO OUT,
SO RECITE US A PSALM.

DON'T DEBATE,
JUST NUMERATE,
THE MONTH AND DATE
OF THIS QUALM.

MY EYES
BEGIN TO CLOSE,
WHILE HE'S SINGING A HYMN.

HE COMMENCED
TO PREACHING,
TEACHINGS,
AND I WAS DREAMING OF THEM.

WITH MY HANDS FULLY CLASPED,
I WAS SPEAKING AMEN.

THE BOMBS
FINAL TICK IGNITED,
BLEACH OFF MY SINS.

AN ANGEL
HAD DESCEND,
SHOWING ME
WHAT'S THE END.

OF A LIFE,
FILLED WITH MISERY,
SO I MADE AN AMENDS.

MY THOUGHTS
FILL THESE PAPERS
AND I PEN A NEW TREND.

SPARKING SMILES ACROSS SOME FACES,
GIVING ME A REASON TO GRIN.
WITH HOPES
IN ALL SINCERITY,
THAT YOU WILL BE A TRUE FRIEND.

THIS IS A NEW BEGINNING,
WHICH IS FAR FROM THE END.

I THANK YOU FOR YOUR TIME,
VALERIE,
ERIC,
SALIM,
AND IRVING.

FOR SURELY,
OPENING DOORS,
SHOWING ME THE WAY IN.

CPSIA information can be obtained at www.ICGtesting.com
Printed in the USA
LVOW12s2141211013

357980LV00007B/253/P